Amazing Life Cycles

CREEPY CRAWLIES

John Allan

The Rhinoceros Beetle is the largest beetle in the world. The male beetles have signature horns on the top of their head, very similar to a rhinoceros.

Contents

ISBN 978 1 912108 091

First published in Great Britain in 2019 by
Hungry Tomato Ltd, The Old Bakery Studios, Blewetts Wharf,
Malpas Road, Truro, Cornwall, TR1 1QH, UK

Manufactured in the United States of America

Words that look **bold like this** are in the glossary.

What is an insect?

***Insects are a group of animals which include bees, butterflies, ants, and beetles. All insects have six legs and a body in three parts. The sections of an insect's body are called the head, the* thorax*, and the* abdomen.**

Insects can be tiny like an ant or big like this giant grasshopper.

Insects use their antennae to smell, touch, and find out what is going on around them.

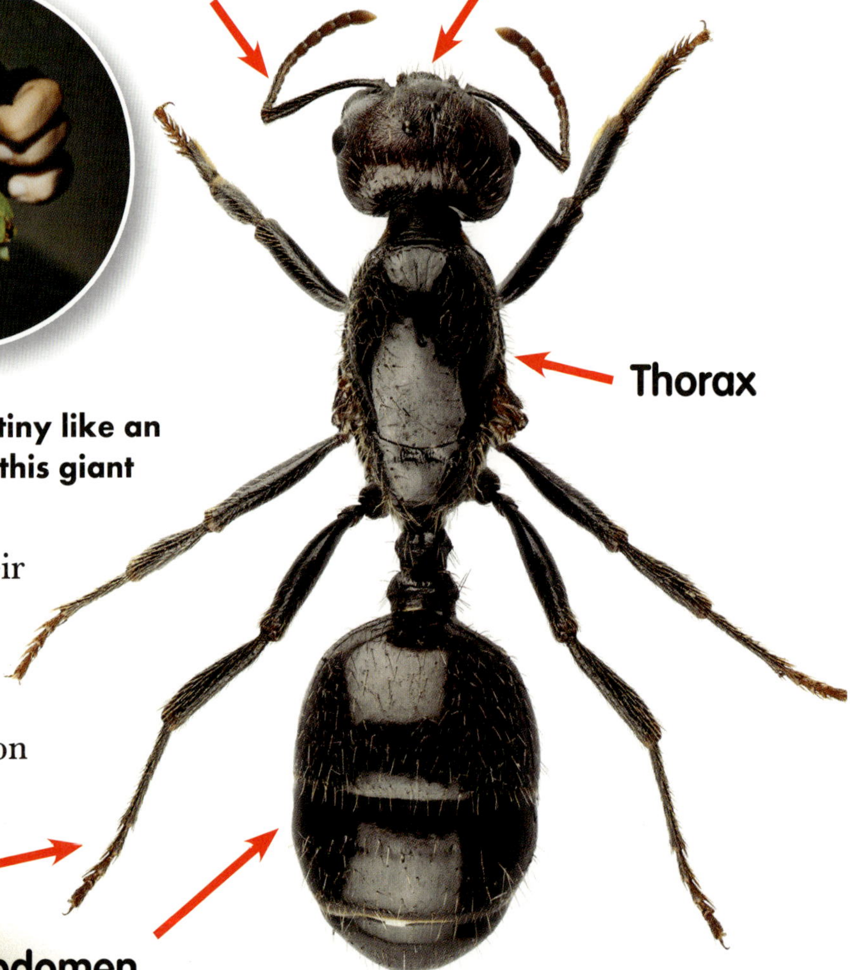

Insects have a pair of feelers, called **antennae**, on their heads.

This is a close-up photo of an ant.

A dragonfly

Many insects, such as dragonflies, have two pairs of wings. Others have one pair of wings, and some insects have no wings.

A fly has one pair of wings.

AMAZING MINIBEAST FACT

There are more types of insects on Earth than any other animals. There are about one million different insects!

A flea has no wings.

Insects have compound eyes. Their eyes are made of many small light-gathering sections.

Insect life

Butterflies have a tongue like a straw for sipping nectar.

***Some insects eat only plants. Others hunt and eat other insects. Wasps, bees, and butterflies are attracted to brightly colored flowers where they drink a sweet juice called* nectar.**

Some insects, such as ants, live in big **colonies**. Others, such as adult stag beetles (shown here), live alone. Adult males and females get together to **mate**.

Many insects eat dead wood from rotting trees. The young, or **larvae**, of stag beetles eat rotting wood.

A firefly

AMAZING MINIBEAST FACT

Some insects use flashes of light, made by special parts under their bodies, to attract a mate.

Female moths produce special smells to attract mates. After mating, the female moth lays lots of eggs. She then leaves the eggs to hatch on their own.

Some insects, such as aphids, can give birth to live young.

What is a spider?

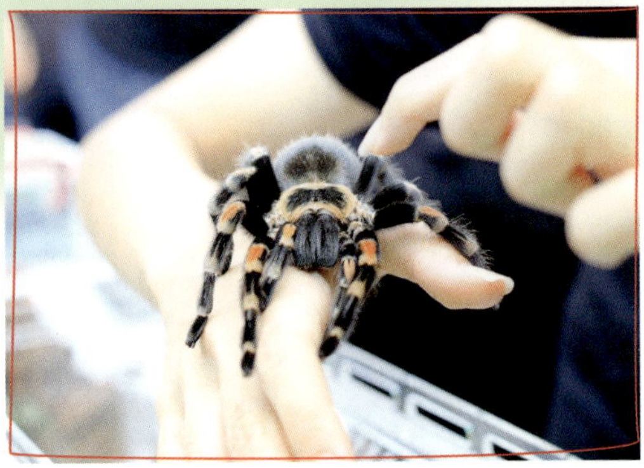

Spiders belong to an animal group called arachnids. All spiders have four pairs of legs and a body in two parts. Spiders are* predators. *They hunt and eat other animals for food.

Tarantulas are big hairy spiders. They use some of the hairs to sense food and predators.

The spider's head and thorax are joined together. This front part of its body is called the prosoma.

Spiders have two small limbs called palps. They use them for feeling things.

The spider's abdomen contains its **digestive organs** and the special glands, or body parts, that make silk for building webs.

AMAZING MINIBEAST FACT

Most spiders have eight eyes. All spiders have **fangs** for injecting poison into their **prey**.

This jumping spider has caught a fly and is holding it using its fangs.

Some spiders build webs. They make them out of silk threads. The threads come out of a part of the spider's body called a spinneret.

Spider life

Although very thin, spider silk is very strong!

There are about 35,000 different types of spiders. Webs are a good sign that spiders are around. Webs made by orb spiders can be found on plants, on fences, and inside buildings.

Some spiders sit in the middle of the web and wait for prey to arrive.

The spider wraps its prey in silk.

Other spiders hide, and when their web begins to shake, they know an insect has become trapped in it.

AMAZING MINIBEAST FACT

Spider silk is liquid (runny) until it comes out of the spinneret.

Trapdoor spiders make underground **burrows** with a door above. When the spider feels something moving close to the door, it jumps out and pulls its prey down into the hole.

Adult spiders live on their own. Males and females only get together to mate. After mating, the female spider lays lots of eggs and covers them with silk.

Many female spiders leave their eggs. The baby spiders hatch and have to take care of themselves.

This nursery web spider carries her eggs with her in a silk egg sac.

Creepy crawly habitats

There can be 2,000 different insects living in a garden.

A habitat is the place where a plant or an animal lives. Insects live in habitats from hot* deserts *to cold mountains. Spiders live in lots of habitats too, but not in very cold places, such as the Arctic or Antarctica.

The ocean is a habitat, but no insects or spiders live in the ocean.

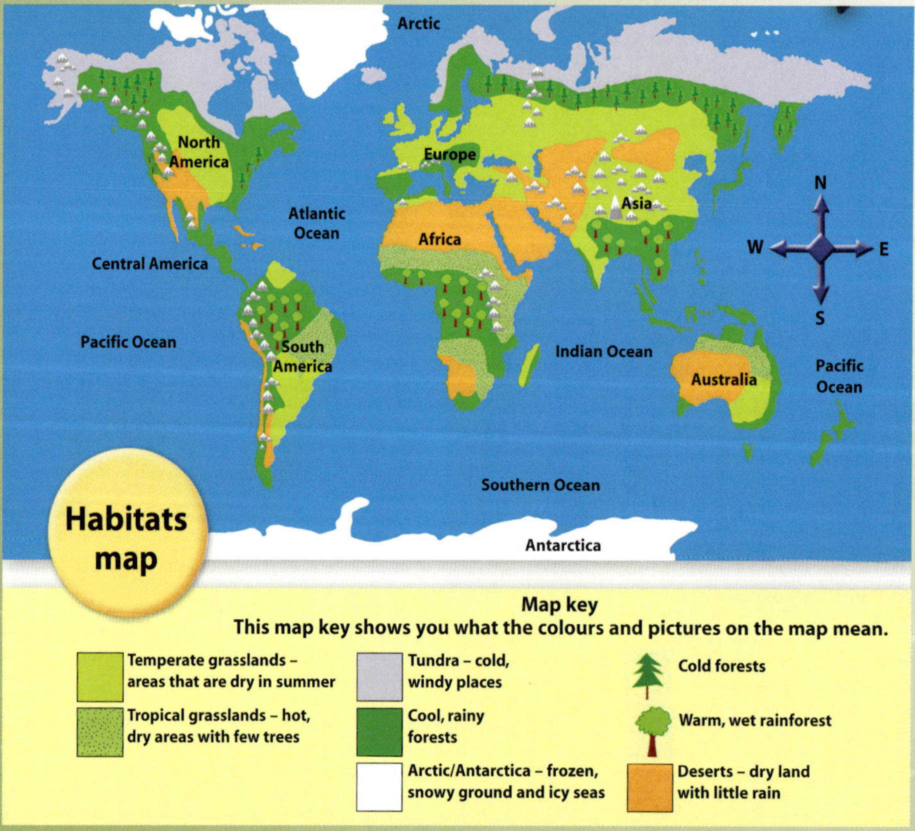

Many insects, such as dragonflies, live in or near **freshwater** pools, rivers and lakes.

AMAZING MINIBEAST FACT

Rainforests have more insects than any other habitat in the world.

Dragonflies lay their eggs in ponds.

One of the reasons there are so many insects and spiders is because they are small animals and do not need much habitat to live in.

Leaf-cutter ants live in South American rainforests.

Hundreds of different types of insects can live on one oak tree.

What is a life cycle?

A life cycle is all the different* stages *and changes that a plant or animal goes through in its life. The diagrams on these pages show an example of an insect life cycle and a spider life cycle.

LADYBIRD BEETLE LIFE CYCLE

Many insects have a life cycle with these stages.

1

A male and female ladybird meet and mate.

2

The female ladybird lays lots of eggs. She doesn't look after the eggs or her babies.

3

A larva hatches from each egg. The larva eats lots of aphids. Then the larva makes a case around its body and becomes a pupa.

4

Inside the case the larva turns into an adult ladybird. This ladybird has just climbed out of its pupal case.

SPIDER LIFE CYCLE

Many spiders have a life cycle with these stages.

1

An adult male and female spider meet and mate.

2

The female lays her eggs in a silk egg sac. Some spiders guard their eggs, others leave them.

3

The spiderlings hatch. Some spiderlings make a tangled web. The spiderlings grow bigger. Their hard outer skin gets too small.

4

The spiderlings molt—their old skin falls off and there's new skin underneath. They molt four or five times before they are fully grown.

Sometimes a female spider thinks a male is prey in her web and eats him!

AMAZING MINIBEAST LIFE CYCLE

Locust

There can be 50 billion desert locusts in one swarm.

Locusts can eat a huge field of wheat in minutes! In a single day a swarm of desert locusts can eat four times as much food as all the humans living in London.

After mating, a female locust pushes her body deep into the soil. She lays 100 eggs one after the other. Female insects lay their eggs through a tube called an ovipositor.

AMAZING MINIBEAST FACT
Female locusts make a sort of foam that protects their eggs.

Tiny locust larvae called nymphs, or hoppers, hatch from the eggs.

As the hoppers grow, their skin becomes too tight. It splits and drops off (as shown above). This is called molting. There is new skin underneath.

After they have molted five times, the young hoppers become adults with wings.

Praying mantis

AMAZING MINIBEAST LIFE CYCLE

Praying mantises have triangular heads.

Praying mantises live in warm places where there are lots of plants. They have very good eyesight and spiny front legs that snap shut on their prey.

AMAZING MINIBEAST FACT

Female mantises are bigger than males. After mating the male must get away quickly in case the female eats him!

They are called praying mantises because they rest with their front legs held together as if they are praying.

After mating, the female mantis lays her eggs. She makes an egg case from a foam that hardens and protects the eggs.

Nymph

Mantis nymphs hatch from the eggs. They are the size of ants.

The female sticks the egg case to a twig, the bark of a tree, or a rock.

At first the nymphs eat small insects such as fruit flies, but as they grow, they eat larger prey.

This giant Asian mantis is eating a cricket!

AMAZING MINIBEAST LIFE CYCLE

Rhinoceros beetle

The rhinoceros, or rhino, beetle lives in rainforests. This beetle gets its name from its horn that looks like a rhino's horn!

Only male rhino beetles have a horn.

AMAZING MINIBEAST FACT

Adult rhino beetles feed on nectar, rotting fruit and **sap** from trees and plants.

After mating, the female rhino beetle lays her eggs. The eggs hatch into larvae. After two to three years, each larva becomes a **pupa**.

A rhino beetle larva eats rotting wood and dead leaves.

Inside its pupal case, the larva turns into an adult rhino beetle. This takes about four to six weeks.

Male rhino beetles sometimes use their horns to fight over **territory** with other males. If the male has a good territory with plenty of food, he will be able to attract a female.

AMAZING MINIBEAST LIFE CYCLE

Birdwing butterfly

This butterfly's wingspan is bigger than the wingspan of some birds!

Butterflies live in lots of different habitats – from rainforests to city gardens. There are about 17,000 different types of butterflies. The Queen Alexandra birdwing is the biggest butterfly in the world.

A male and female butterfly meet and mate. The female lays lots of eggs. Larvae, called caterpillars, hatch from the eggs. They eat and eat.

Then the caterpillar makes a case around its body and becomes a pupa.

All butterflies have the same kind of life cycle.

Female

Male

The male and female Queen Alexandra birdwing butterflies look different to each other. The female is bigger than the male.

The caterpillar gets too big for its skin. The old skin molts and there's a new skin underneath. The caterpillar molts several times.

Inside the pupal case, the caterpillar becomes a butterfly!

AMAZING MINIBEAST LIFE CYCLE

Spider-hunting wasp

A spider-hunting wasp sting can be very painful to humans.

There are about 4,000 different types of spider-hunting wasps in the world. The female wasp will fly above the ground or run about tapping the ground with her antennae hunting for spiders.

When the female wasp catches a spider, she fights with the spider and stings it so it is paralysed. This means it cannot move, but it is still alive.

The wasp then drags the spider to a burrow she has dug and pulls the spider underground.

The paralyzed spider cannot escape.

The female lays a single egg on the spider and then seals the burrow. When the egg hatches, the young wasp larva eats the spider alive!

The wasp larva spins a silk case called a cocoon. Inside the cocoon it becomes an adult wasp. The new adult wasp crawls to the surface and escapes from the burrow.

AMAZING MINIBEAST LIFE CYCLE

Jumping spider

Most jumping spiders have hairy bodies.

Jumping spiders live in forests, in woodlands, in gardens, and in many other habitats around the world. There are about 5,000 different types of jumping spiders.

The jumping spider in this photo is pouncing on a hover fly. The spider attaches a safety line of silk in case it misses its landing spot.

Jumping spiders jump to catch prey, and to escape from predators, such as birds.

After mating the female jumping spider lays lots of eggs in one go. She wraps them in an egg sac made of silk thread.

The female guards her eggs until the spiderlings hatch.

Jumping spiders have eight eyes— two of the eyes are very big like car headlights. The spider's big eyes help it to spot its insect prey, and judge the distance of its jump.

This jumping spider is about to eat a cricket.

Water spider

The water spider lives underwater in ponds or slow-flowing rivers. It lives in a diving bell, like a bubble, made out of silk which it fills with air.

Large water spiders eat baby fish and tadpoles.

The spider sits inside the diving bell. When insects and other prey pass, the spider rushes out, grabs the prey, and takes it back to the bell to eat.

The spider sits with just its front legs dangling in the water. Its head is in the bell so it can breathe.

The male and female water spider mate inside the female's diving bell.

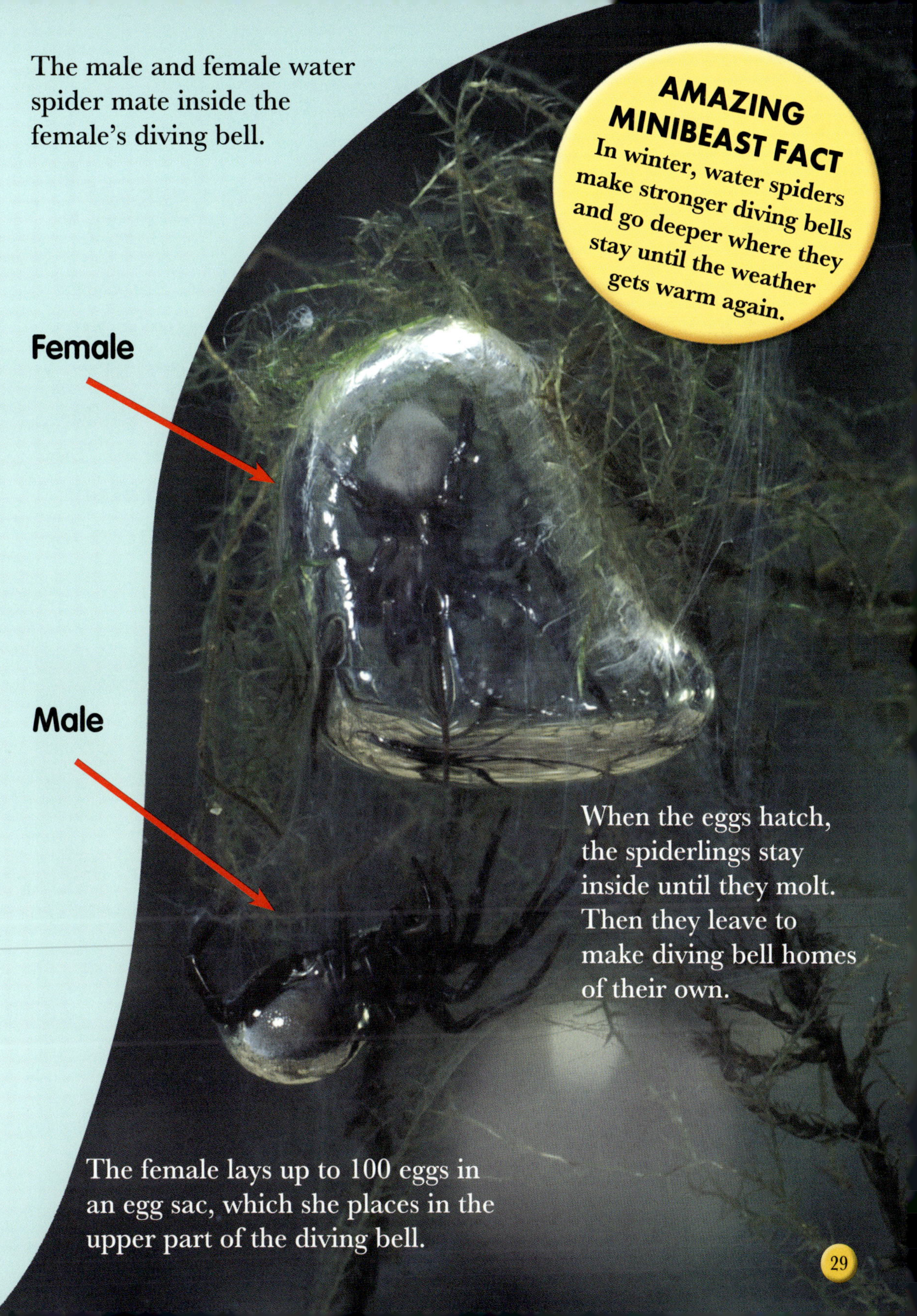

AMAZING MINIBEAST FACT
In winter, water spiders make stronger diving bells and go deeper where they stay until the weather gets warm again.

When the eggs hatch, the spiderlings stay inside until they molt. Then they leave to make diving bell homes of their own.

The female lays up to 100 eggs in an egg sac, which she places in the upper part of the diving bell.

That's amazing!

The wolf spider carries her spiderlings on her back.

Most insects and spiders do not care for their eggs or young, but there are some amazing minibeast parents. These moms feed their babies and protect them from being eaten by predators.

Insects such as bees and wasps live in large groups and make a nest in which to look after their young.

A female earwig looks after her eggs inside an underground burrow. She licks them every day to stop fungus from growing on them.

A female queen wasp is building a nest to lay her eggs. An egg is laid in each cell of the nest. Larvae hatch from the eggs.

AMAZING MINIBEAST FACT

Female paper wasps feed their larvae on chewed up insects.

Paper wasps make a nest of papery chewed up wood.

The other females in the group, called workers, help to look after the nest and feed the larvae.

Glossary

abdomen – the part of an animal's body that contains the digestive organs
antennae – a pair of feelers used by an insect to touch and smell its environment
burrows – tunnels and holes under the ground where some animals live
colonies – large groups
deserts – very dry places, that are often sandy or rocky. Deserts can be very hot in the day. Some deserts get cold at night.
digestive organs – the body parts that digest food, such as the stomach
fangs – very sharp teeth.
freshwater – rainwater, and the water in ponds and some rivers. It is not salty.
fungus – a very simple living thing that grows and spreads. Another word we use for some types of fungus is mold.
larvae – the young of some insects
mate – when a male and female animal meet and have babies
nectar – a sweet liquid inside flowers
predators – animals which hunt and kill other animals for food
prey – animals which are hunted by other animals as food
pupa – the stage in the life cycle of some insects between a larva and an adult
sap – a liquid in trees and plants
stages – different times of an animal's life when the animal changes
territory – an area or place where an animal feeds, mates and has its young
thorax – the middle part of an insect's body. The legs and wings are attached to the thorax.

Index

Picture credits

Shutterstock. 1: Stuart Hamilton. 2-3: Marek R Swadzba. 4-5: Cristina Romero Palma, diko_163, Hintau Aliaksei, Cosmin Mancini, Rudmer Zwerver, Garo Manjikian. 6-7: Atom Wang, Dieter Herrmann, Khlung Center, Frances van der Merwe. 8-9: Narin Nonthamand, Vitalii Hulai, Cathy Keifer, Eugene Kalenkovich. 10-11: bbbb, Jarp2, Pong Wira, Ulum Miftahul, Sandra Stanbridge. 12-13: Romacho, Eric Iseeleee, Zerbor. 14-15: SonNUmber4, Brett Hondow, Eduardo Estellez, Antermite, Tomatito, ARCAN, Sarah2, Tviolet. 16-17: Awei, Texturis. 18-19: Peter Waters, Narupon Nimpaidboon, Cathy Keifer. 20-21: NH, Lightboxx, WOnderisland, Govorov Evgeny, Davit Buachidze. 22-23: Matee Nuserm, Mathisa, Butterfly Hunter. 24-25: Yerbolat Shadrakhof, D. Kucharski. Ian Redding, Jean Whitney, Simon_g. 26-27: Sebastian Janiki, Pichit Sansupa, Annop Youngrot. 28-29: Javi Roces. 30-31: Miles Boyer, Ian Redding, McCarthy's Photoworks, Kelly Marken.